POEMS

FROM A CABIN ON BIG SUR

ALSO BY PETER THABIT JONES

Poetry

Tacky Brow (Outposts Publications, U.K., 1974)
The Apprenticeship (Cwm Nedd Press, U.K., 1977)
Clocks Tick Differently (Celtion Poetry Series, U.K., 1980)
Visitors (Poetry Wales Press, U.K., 1986)
The Cold Cold Corner (Dark Lane Poetry, U.K., 1995)
Ballad of Kilvey Hill (Swansea Bay Publishers/Eastside Poetry, U.K., 1999)
The Lizard Catchers
(Cross-Cultural Communications, U.S.A., 2006/reprinted 2007 & 2008)
POET TO POET #1: Bridging the Waters: Swansea to Sag Harbor,
with American poet Vince Clemente
(Cross-Cultural Communications, U.S.A.,
& The Seventh Quarry Press, U.K., 2008)
Whispers of the Soul, with American poet Vince Clemente
(a bilingual collection: English-Romanian, Translated by Dr. Olimpia Iacob)
(Editura Fundatiei Poezia Iasi, Romania, 2008)
The Boy and the Lion's Head
(a verse drama, bilingual: English-Romanian,
Translated by Dr. Olimpia Iacob)
(Citadela Publishing, Romania, 2009)

Prose

Broken Tin and Other Stories (Castaway Press, U.K., 1979
Dylan Thomas Walking Tour of Greenwich Village, New York,
with Aeronwy Thomas
(for the Wales International Centre, New York/Welsh
Assembly Government, 2008)
www.walesworldnation.com
PODCAST: www.dylanthomaswalkingtourmp3.com.

PETER THABIT JONES

POEMS

FROM A CABIN ON BIG SUR

Cross-Cultural Communications
Merrick, New York
2011

Editor-Publisher: **Stanley H. Barkan**

Cross-Cultural Communications
239 Wynsum Avenue
Merrick, New York 11566-4725 USA
Tel: (516) 868-5635 / Fax: (516) 379-1901
cccpoetry@aol.com
www.cross-culturalcommunications.com

Library of Congress Control Number: 2011920458

Cloth Edition/ISBN 978-0-89304-575-3
Paper Edition/ISBN 978-0-89304-576-0

Text Photos of Peter Thabit Jones
by Melissa Goese-Goble, Patricia Holt, Carolyn Mary Kleefeld,
and Linda Parker

Back Cover Photo of Peter Thabit Jones
by Linda Parker

First Edition

Designed by Tchouki
Printed in the United States of America

For Carolyn Mary Kleefeld, poet and artist, who made this collection possible; and my heartfelt thanks for her friendship and for an inspiring and inspired month as her poet-in-residence in her wonderful cabin, The Rainbow Room, on Big Sur, California, for the whole of May in 2010.

My special thanks to Patricia Holt for her friendship, and for her assistance in bringing this collection to publication.

Thanks, too, to Linda Parker, John Larson, and Laura Zabrowski for their friendship, for ensuring that all went well during my stay in the cabin, and for making me feel so welcome during my visit.

Thanks also to John Dotson for his friendship and his assistance with this collection.

Lastly, my gratitude to American poet and Emeritus Professor Vince Clemente and my American publisher Stanley H. Barkan, also a poet, for their constant support and encouragement over the years.

CONTENTS

Peter in Front of Big Sur Mountains

PREFACE

In May 2010, I was invited to spend a whole month as poet-in-residence in a cabin on Big Sur. The offer came from Carolyn Mary Kleefeld, a poet and artist whose powerful work is infused with the incredible landscape of her home nestling above the life-force of the Pacific Ocean.

I left Swansea, Wales, with the intention of completing a new drama, encouraged by the fact that my recently published verse drama, *The Boy and the Lion's Head*, would have its world-premiere performance in Monterey, whilst I was in California. It was to be directed by dramatist, poet, and sculptor John Dotson, who lives in Carmel.

I did not anticipate the profound impact that the landscape and Carolyn and her team (Patricia Holt, Linda Parker, John Larson, and Laura Zabrowski) would have on my writing. The poems came quickly and naturally. I went on daily walks, alone, letting the island-like world seep into my very being; and I went on walks with Carolyn, where we had long and fascinating talks on literature and life. She also placed books in the cabin for me to read at leisure. Two, De Casseres' book on Spinoza and his own *Chameleon, Being a Book of My Selves*, were a revelation to me. I also re-read her *Climates of the Mind* and *The Alchemy of Possibility*, works that shine with her engaging intelligence and her sense of 'shoots of everlastingness'.*

The beauty of the place was also tinged with the real life-force, what seemed like a constant, Pacific-powered wind that bullied the cabin and the spread-out forest of trees behind it. For me, it added to my perception that I was living on the edge of the world, on a nerve of nature itself.

Great writers have written about Big Sur; my contribution is more humble. It is the record of a man who was born and grew up in the working-class area of Eastside Swansea, the 'ugly' part of Dylan Thomas' 'ugly, lovely town'; a man whose only access as a boy to the life-force was Kilvey Hill, which sulked above the home he shared with his dying grandfather and nurse of a grandmother. A man who suddenly, at the age of fifty-nine years, found himself in paradise; and a man who indeed discovered Edward Thomas was right when he wrote, 'I cannot bite the day to the core'.

—**Peter Thabit Jones**

June 2010

---

* *'shoots of everlastingness'* —from "The Retreat" by Henry Vaughan.

The Cabin in Big Sur

ON READING PETER THABIT JONES'S
Poems from a Cabin on Big Sur

Born and raised in Swansea, Wales, Peter Thabit Jones teaches literature courses at the Adult Education Department at Swansea University, and an additional literature course at 5 Cwmdonkin Drive, birthplace of Dylan Thomas.

In a letter addressed to me dated July 2010, just home from his "Fourth American poetry tour," culminating as poet-in-residence for a month, at the invitation of poet and friend Carolyn Mary Kleefeld, in a solitary cabin "on" Big Sur, high above the Pacific Ocean, Peter wrote:

> I enclose the typed manuscript of my poems from a cabin on Big Sur. You are the first person to see it. I have titled On, rather than In because the cabin was on a mountain cliff overlooking the Pacific Ocean, the man on Big Sur reunited with the boy on Kilvey [the towering hill above his Swansea home].

> It was a religious/spiritual experience for me, as I, Peter Thabit Jones, was diminished in the huge life-force that confronted me daily. God grew and grew, and the universe unfolded in all its amazing pattern of glory. The man on Big Sur saw/observed with the eyes of maturity, but he felt with the open heart of the boy on Kilvey.

Indeed, the month-long retreat in this "monk's cell" of a cabin sanctuary is reverentially chronicled in this manuscript. I truly feel anointed as I read through its sixty-eight poems and concluding "Coda." I love the poems' clarity of vision, this genuflecting before a life-affirming experience, part of the webwork of a world, so much in its purity, like that of the very dawn of Creation.

The poems vary, both in length and in prosody, yet always with Peter's dual vision and sensibility: "The man on Big Sur [observing] with the eyes of maturity, but [feeling] with the open heart of the boy on Kilvey."

About the volume's initial poem, "The Airport in San Francisco," Peter tells me in the July 2010 letter: "The opening poem/experience about the boy in the airport, a boy named Mathew, set the tone of my mind for my four weeks of virtual solitude." Of course, it is also the name of his lost son, Mathew, found dead in his crib at eight months old, a loss Peter carries with him daily, attempts, somehow, to come to terms with this soul-deep wound in poems like "The Cold, Cold Corner" (from *The Lizard Catchers*, Cross-Cultural Communications, 2006), a six-part elegy for a son he will never see again. I'd like to quote just two sections from this poem: "3. Mathew," and "6. Remembrance." We understand, then, how this spontaneous call in an airport, for a "toddler," one who "runs from his mother" indeed for Peter, "set the tone" for his four weeks of "virtual solitude" in Big Sur.

3. Mathew

On Sundays, we go to attend to his grave:
The large, paper cornet foaming with flowers;
And our eyes as dry as the surrounding stones.
His smile and small darkness are vinegar
Memories stinging the cut cord of our living love.
His white cross stabs the formal grass. His photos,
Wordless elegies, inhabit my wallet.

6. Remembrance

I bury you softly in thoughts like snow.
I wear my grief, my black flower of pain.
My thoughts are prayers that can never reach home;
I tend to your grave in the cold of cold rain.

And to think, nonchalantly in "The Airport in San Francisco," along with lamenting Peter, we hear, indeed, eavesdrop " 'Mathew!' she calls / 'Mathew!' // And lights / A dry bonfire / Deep in my heart": one, I fear, burning to this day, for he confides, "A shadow in the soul, / Two syllables of love, / A cross with some words, / The silence of dust." And the "silence" there in that cabin, yet one eternally sanctified.

Another early poem, one of incipient moments, "Arrival the Cabin, Big Sur: First Night," only has five lines, yet is so typically the voice of the poet of the full volume, always this sonic-semantic integrity, reverence for both vision of the natural world and the levitating sanctity of words:

The ocean washes
The winds of my dreams. I sleep
At the feet of its roars,
The engine of its life-force;
The eternal Pacific.

And in the many poems that capture Peter's solemn walks along "The eternal Pacific," solitary or with "adopted sister" Carolyn, one is reminded of Emerson's comment about Thoreau, how "The length of his walk uniformly determined the length of his line." We find such a definition of Self in "Walking with Carolyn," inspired by their initial evening walk together, with "The Pacific purring / Its aeons below us." This is a poem of finely hewn couplets, each line becoming a footprint along the ocean's tideline.

From our oceans of thoughts.
A man and a woman,

We follow our shadows.
Our words burn their passion

On rough drafts of the wind.
At the edge of your world,

These very ambulatory "rough drafts" became the poems of this volume, as we come upon in "Writing in the Cabin," the poet at work on his poems, those, as he tells us in the Dedication, written "in memory of my father / who still sails the ocean of my heart," the very father lost at sea, Peter just a boy at the time. We find him alone at his modest table "Writing, stopping, / Thinking, writing." And along with his finely crafted tercets, we hear these antiphonal cadences that chime with hymnal sanctity throughout this poem of creation, one that, "Rides through each day / To the language and the longing / Of the Earth's growing song;. . ." And the imagery itself, always from the sounds, fragrances, rhythms of his sea-surging life, here, worlds from Swansea, yet still the boy under Kilvey Hill.
   And in "Morning," after he wakes, ". . . so tired / From a night of writing," he finds just under him, and certain as grace is certain, "The ocean still leaving / Its verbs on the shore;. . ." indeed this act of faith, in what he tells us, "was a religious/spiritual experience," yet one enshrined in this very world.

And always this "length of the walk," as the volume is prolific with poems, at least a dozen, of ambulatory, soul-seeking wanderings along the ocean's tide line, the woods beyond the cabin, each walk shrouded in Time and the lingering caul of mist that is Big Sur. Early in the volume we come upon a cluster of three short tightly braided such poems: "Evening Walk: One," "Evening Walk: Two," and "Morning Walk." In the initial poem, we are with the poet "Above the sea-pounded bay / That's kingfisher-blue,. . ." Then this leap to Faith, immersion in self, one plaited to the natural world, "It seems I'm on an island / A poet now castaway."

By the third poem in the cluster, he is so immersed in the mystical calling that is Big Sur, that he has entered what Japanese Zen poets call Yasen kanna, translated as "alone at night in a boat," shedding the self, becoming a pulsating particle of the natural world.

In "Black Scarab on the Path," we come upon, with Peter, an isolated, possibly lost "black scarab" or huge beetle. The poet, so absorbed in the image of this, also ambulatory creature of nature, and not unlike himself, asks: "What's its concept of being / Under the enormous stars?" And he continues observing and questioning: "What keeps it going / Through obstacles of the night?" Peter's conclusion is one all-embracing for human, animal, even planetary life, there in the orchards of the spheres: "Is it a sense of its home / Where something's waiting like love?"

And in "Pacific Ocean," one for his wife, Hilary, alone in Swansea, "home," where something is waiting for love, we hear from our "castaway" here on "This daily walk / That takes me / Far from 'home',. . ." the very "scratch" of his footprints as he confronts the sea, indeed at this moment in his life, this very fount, "Which leaves its grief / Along a broken shore,. . ." yet there, both as life's solemn evanescence, and living presence of life's Enigma, this sacred union of Temporal and Eternal, unfolding. We must conclude that each walk, in spite of place, time, distance, is part of life's hallowed rite of passage.

Many of these poems are also paeans of poignant indebtedness for Peter's Big Sur companions, comforting presences during that month of pious reflection and self-discovery. And only fitting we begin with one for Carolyn, at work as a painter, her secluded, open-air studio, just behind her Big Sur home. In "Carolyn Painting: *The Absurd Hero*" we find her at work in this ". . . patch of garden / Where Buddhas rest / In contemplation." Her painter's world is not unlike Peter's, one tinctured with the Zen notion of Yasen kanna, one where he can ". . . reach and almost cup / A lone grey boat in my hand." For just below Carolyn ". . . the ocean pulls / Its slow full song,. . ." We also are privy to her world, where, "Birds stir and flowers flare, / As the sun behind her / Fingers its colours / Over the calm sea, . . ."

And Peter pays homage to Benjamin De Casseres, whose books Carolyn placed in the cabin for him to read. The line in De Casseres' *Chame-*

leon, *Being a Book of My Selves*, "We go toward ourselves" is epigraph for "Birthday Poem: The Boy and the Man," this balanced psychic drama, again, prayer-like in antiphonal cadences, as "The boy on Kilvey / Is the man on Big Sur;..." the meditation, this birth of two who indeed "... go toward ourselves."

It is the prosody that gives this poem its enduring nature, lines of balanced, parallel cadences both stirring and subtle, yet as lucid as the waters below Peter's cabin on Big Sur, or those girding the Swansea home of his boyhood. After the initial two lines, assertion of this "boy/man" union, miraculously, here on Big Sur, we hear how Peter's prayer-like intonations come to rest in the reader's larder of heart: "Both humbled by the land / And the sea's vast engine; / Both letting the clouds / Start thoughts in their mind; / Both feeling the trees / Root into their tongue; ..." The poem continues its sonic-semantic depiction of "birth," of prior divided selves, now in this sacred fount, these very amniotic fluids of their "shared" Big Sur days. And with them always, this consoling presence of a God-head: "Both blown by a wind / Like the breath of a god;..." And finally, indeed this act of faith, again with in the aural boundaries of these haunting, chapel-hushed, musical phrasings, "Both dressing their ghosts / With the songs from their heart." After reading such a poem, one is inclined to murmur, "Amen."

In another paean to Peter's Big Sur companions, "Your Blue Eyes Call Me" (dedicated to Patricia Holt), we find the poem at rest in eleven finely woven tercets, some with full rhyme, others with antiphonal repletion of initial lines. We discover such prosody there to gird, accompany, the poem's bold leap back in Time, as we hear in the initial tercet:

> Your blue eyes
> Call me
> Back to Atlantis;

And about "Atlantis," this symbolic island supposed to have existed, self-possessed there in the western sea, indeed an ideal world, richly developed civilization, and one that intrigued Plato. The legend-impregnated human imagination, as its demise, thousands of years ago, was the result of an "earthquake." Atlantis, its slow drift through time, remains this near-perfect utopian world, one now, come to rest in Big Sur, embedded there, and as Peter intones "Your blue eyes / Call me / To a world // We have lost; ..."

And I am trancelike reading this poem, as its diction is truly unique to the volume, as Peter places us in a world, "Where seahorses / Rode / An ecstatic dream;..." indeed such a visionary world, "Where our thoughts / Were like rainbows / That necklace the sun;..." And he only deepens the poem's elo - quence with "Where the golden days / Danced with the souls / Of our world;..."

Whatever he found in Big Sur, that modest cabin above the Pacific, a serene, trance-like world, and as he concludes in a hushed, reverential silence, "To a place / We have lost / Except // For the feelings / In memory's / Dust." As for "In memory's / Dust,. . ." I feel he again evokes the memory of his lost infant son Mathew, one to become "A shadow in the soul / Two syllables of love, / A cross with some words, / The silence of dust." This is our poet, Peter Thabit Jones, with such a grasp of poetic prosody, far-reaching human devotion to words, all nurtured by a reverence for life, the human family.

Another poem of enshrinement for those in Big Sur, Peter's "companions" along the journey that taught him "We go towards ourselves," is one called "Big Sur Sculptor Edmund Kara's Derelict Cabin." Peter calls the cabin "A shrine of dark wood," and visits daily, I am sure, in homage to this brooding embodiment of life's pronounced impermanence.

The poem is made up of seven irregular, unrhyming stanzas, as winding as the path "Once worn by your shadow." And the path ends in "Your workshop lodged / Just above the Pacific." This daily descent has the quality of pilgrimage, as this "derelict cabin" "At this world where you worked" is now splintered by time and elements of the sea-surging world, just below. It should be said, however, Edmund Kara remains in the cabin's fibers of disintegration, as "Fragments of the windows / Litter the deck floor. / They're as sharp as the tools / You once used to shape / Truths into wood: / And wood into truths." The elegy concludes with the man, his self-imposed fate, his days, indeed cast in life's ultimate relinquishment, this ". . . recluse, / Shunning art's game / And the ego's long thirst,. . ." And as the poet understands in the deep- est recesses of the heart, the man, Edmund Kara, is finally "Like a castaway / On an island / Alone with his dream." We, along with Peter, are then privy to the very nature of human existence, of Time's bold dichotomous nature, the temporal wed to the eternal.

Approaching the volume's conclusion is the poem, "The Cabin," one "for Vince Clemente," for some reason, and I feel undeserved, as I was not in Big Sur as one of Peter's steadying companions, but did in one of my letters, describe his writer's sanctuary-retreat as a "Monk's cell." We find Peter indeed in "A monk's cell, wooden, / Squatting above the ocean, / Big Sur's shattered coast." And just below him, hallowed presence of a world, always this, "religious/spiritual experience," and details of this nurturing, impregnating life, all like "The stained-glass blue sea," such a metaphoric leap, yet so like our poet's prosody, always this bold clarity of vision and experience. And nothing escapes him, as each day we see "Jigsaw-piece cliffs, proud mountains / Touching gathered clouds" and, he shifts angle of vision, as ". . . the window's picture / Is shadowed"; with "the sea, // The cliffs, the mountains, charcoaled / By the cloud of night; . . ." Even this cloak of

16

darkness only makes more poignant the world just below his "monk's cell," the poet, indeed reverential, one forever solemn, held in the amniotic fluids of ". . . waves coming / To gasp on the shore."

And now just before the volume's "Coda," this final look, attempt at summing up, put to rest and carry forever in the larder of the heart, these hallowed days, we hear Peter in "Leaving," the volume's penultimate poem: "As I pack to leave / It all seems so unreal; . . . // In this cabin / On Big Sur, / On the shelf / Of an ocean,. . ." And about this "ocean," he will forever hear it, "Endlessly weaving / Its haunting rhythms, / Endlessly making / Its mind-moving myth."

The Coda is made up of two poems, "1. The Sea of Big Sur" and "2. Thoughts on the Way to San Francisco Airport." The Coda is always this consummation, in both music and literature, of primary, thematic, and structural elements in a work, often disparate, yet somehow finally woven together in this now seamless composition or text. In "The Sea of Big Sur," Peter attempts a true summing up, with echoes of the volume's poems, diction, at times colloquial and informal, at times "surging" in its eloquence, echoes of themes and character, as "The sighs of fathers / And sons rise / From below / To bellow and blow / In the loveless night. . . ." undoubtedly resurrection of Peter's sea-lost father, of son Mathew.

What we have here, in these poems of sonic-semantic summation, is a physical/spiritual assertion and acceptance, as if in a genuflection gesture, of Life's Enigma, its simultaneity of birth and ultimate death. And the key word here is acceptance as Peter returns to Swansea, at peace with such a lived experience, as the poem concludes: 'It is not even a moment / In the mood / Of the mind of creation, / The ocean washing / The bowl of a dream." What he has lived through, this month of May 2010, in that "Cabin on Big Sur" is total Existence in microcosm, yet an anchor to keep him afloat.

And finally, we are back where we began our journey, in "Thoughts on the Way to San Francisco Airport." We find in the poem's final line, what is to be the volume's sought-after truth, Peter's very passacaglia through "Time-Space: Crystallizations of God," simply that, "And being is believing."

After meditating on life's inherent mystery, how, "The mind is a sky / At night, teeming with stars. / Creation's abandoned dream? / Or cells replicating hope?," his conclusion is then this synthesis: the voice of the boy wandering under Kilvey Hill, the man, late in his fifth decade in that Big Sur cabin, above the ocean's eternal sea surge, as "God grew and grew, and the universe unfolded in all its amazing patterns of glory." And now we read full text of the final stanza of this remarkable volume by the poet as courage-teacher:

No stone-built place can
Bring you to your knees.
Time is a shadow of you;
Aeons are moments,
A mere one pulse
To the slow mathematics
Of your each movement;
And being is believing.

And how I pray I have fulfilled my promise to poet Peter Thabit
Jones, asserted in my July 21, 2010 letter, after receiving the manuscript in
which I promised to write a long, critical piece, "sharing with you the Yeats
notion you are wed to, how, "Words alone are certain good." And it is all here
in such a volume of verse, the poet, Peter, as wordsmith, as visionary vessel
of faith, as "being is believing": the poem, always this ideal cage of form,
of braiding of selves, of the very sea surge that is Life's sacrosanct Enigma.

—**Vince Clemente**

September 2010

Peter by a Redwood in Big Sur

THE AIRPORT IN SAN FRANCISCO

Standing in a queue
With my publisher
And his wife,
Tired
As refugees
From our New York flight,
I watch
As a toddler
Runs from his mother.
"Mathew!" she calls,
"Mathew!"

It's the name
Of my son,
Gone thirty-five years
And laid in the earth;
A shadow in the soul,
Two syllables of love,
A cross with some words,
The silence of dust.

"Mathew!" she calls,
"Mathew!"

And lights
A dry bonfire
Deep in my heart.

THE NIGHT BEFORE THE CABIN:
THE WAYSIDE INN HOTEL, CARMEL
(The Woman Next Door, Midnight)

The walls are paper-thin;
Your footsteps walk
The room of my thoughts,
Your night coughs scratch
My body's stillness.

Your day-weary sighs
Die
On the floor of my mind.

ARRIVAL THE CABIN, BIG SUR: FIRST NIGHT

The ocean washes
The winds of my dreams. I sleep
At the feet of its roars,
The engine of its life-force;
The eternal Pacific.

WALKING WITH CAROLYN

We walk the evening
Of our new friendship;

The Pacific purring
Its aeons below us,

The sky the colour
Of heaven above us.

Spinoza, Whitman,
Edward Thomas, and

Your friend Edmund Kara
Are names that bubble up

From our oceans of thoughts.
A man and a woman,

We follow our shadows.
Our words burn their passion

On rough drafts of the wind.
At the edge of your world,

You open the door
To Edmund's work-place,

A shipwreck of a home
Submitting to the sea,

Collapsing to the depths
Of eternity,

As a startled bird shoots
Its way towards freedom.

WRITING IN THE CABIN

(*in memory of my father
who still sails the ocean of my heart*)

I sit at the table;
Writing, stopping,
Thinking, writing.

The so-close ocean
Unfolds its
Sound patterns;

Heavily, rhythmically,
A motion perfected
Since its beginning;

It wears away
What we have called time,
Wears away

At my planning thoughts.
This dream of a shell,
This Big Sur cabin

Rides through each day
To the language and the longing
Of the Earth's growing song;

An unfinished poem
Forever aching
On the shores of the mind.

Writing in the Cabin

MORNING

The dawn makes its presence
Known in the cabin;
Sunlight flames the walls,
The glow of morning.

I wake, so tired
From a night of writing,
The residue of words
Still clogging my thoughts.

Outside, the day opens
Itself to the world;
The ocean still leaving
Its verbs on the shore;

And a litter of birds
Fragmenting one song.

PROVISIONS
(for Laura)

You bring me weekly
Provisions, a mobile-shop
Of sorts; potatoes,
Milk, bread, packed bottled-water,
Some treats (chocolate, beer);
And always a smile,
Direct from Carmel,
A greeting warm as the sun.

GULL ON THE PACIFIC OCEAN

A bobbing white daub
Slowly going its own way
Through the bullying waves.

A Vulture, Big Sur

VULTURES, BIG SUR: AFTERNOON

I walk the dirt path
Above the loud sea
That froths its white gasps
Along the rocked shore,
The tourist in me
Taking quick photos.

Then out of the growth
That banks my slow route,
A large bird escapes
And makes for the sky:
A vulture gliding
With natural menace.

Then one becomes two
And two becomes three;
They startle my heart,
Circling their presence,
As I shoot a stern flash
With my small camera,

And hurry my walking
To the time-eaten cliff.

Two Lizards Outside the Cabin

TWO LIZARDS

Outside the cabin,
My lone monk's cell
For this May month,

Two dark lizards
Frozen on a rock
Baked by the sun.

You and me, love,
Resting together
In our faraway home,

Now a dream beyond
This writing cabin,
Beyond the Big Sur coast.

A View from the Path Below the Cabin

EVENING WALK: ONE

On the sloping path
Above the sea-pounded bay
That's kingfisher-blue,

It seems I'm on an island,
A poet now castaway.

EVENING WALK: TWO

A helicopter,
Blood-red, thunders into view,
Disturbing Big Sur.

MORNING WALK

I stand above the sea,
Like a colossus of Greece,
The sun on my back.
I reach and almost cup
A lone grey boat in my hand.

TRUCK

A white truck rumbles
Into a tunnel of redwoods,
Erasing itself.

AT THE WRITING TABLE

I sit at the table,
With paper and pen;
A blank page disturbs
For almost one hour.

The words are refusing
To sound off for thoughts;
And thoughts are still nesting
In long-ago trees.

Outside the small cabin,
Unpaid and on form,
And relying on
Their centuries of trade,

Some busy birds share
Their bright sprinkling of song.

THREE A.M. PERFORMANCE

The wind and the ocean
Wake me up
As they dance
On a stage
At the edge of the world.

FIRST DAY OF MAY

Day fingers the song
That strikes the moaning
Epitaph of blue.

The fresh wind gargles
A pacified place;
Time burns each moment.

The far sky swallows
A homeward-bound bird;
A fallen acorn

Is a hand-grenade.
Edmund's sad cabin
Aches with its silence.

Lone footsteps punish
A trail of gravel;
Trees sway, drunk with dawn.

A lizard's a brooch
On a patch of dust.
A poet breakfasts

On words of his world.

Carolyn Mary Kleefeld, Poet and Artist,
Painting in Her Garden

CAROLYN PAINTING: *THE ABSURD HERO*

Above Big Sur
On a patch of garden
Where Buddhas rest
In contemplation
And the ocean pulls
Its slow full song,
She stands before
Her work-day easel.

Birds stir and flowers flare,
As the sun behind her
Fingers its colours
Over the calm sea,
And a helicopter
Drones like a bumble bee
Across the blue,
Wide, open sky.

I sit and watch
As she paints and talks;
Her rainbow of ideas
Resting on the palette,
As she serves her vision,
Its light and its shadows,
The brush soothing
A grey and world-weary face.

BLACK SCARAB ON THE PATH

What is a moment
To a black scarab shifting
Slowly on the path?
What's its concept of being
Under the enormous stars?

What is the fear
Burning away at its thoughts?
What keeps it going
Through obstacles of the night?
Is it a sense of its home
Where something's waiting like love?

A NIGHT OUT
(for Susan Zsigmond)

After a fine dinner,
Some drinks
And conversation,

We watch a new film
In the large home
Of Vilmos Zsigmond

Cinematographer,
The Deer Hunter,
The Witches of Eastwick

(The list is endless),
With his wife, Susan,
Your friend and neighbour.

Later, we walk
Through the Big Sur night,
Dark as a cinema;

The crackling soundtrack
Of the ocean
Beyond us,

The stars more searching
Than an
Usherette's torch;

And the movie of life,
The incredible
Illusion,

All around us.

By the Pacific Ocean

PACIFIC OCEAN
(for my wife)

This daily walk
That takes me
Far from 'home',
A gift of a cabin
Squatting on a hill,
Sees me leave
The desk-bound chore behind,
The drama of words
Across a rhythmic page.

My footsteps scratch
A long and dusty path
That trails its way
Just before the sea,
Which leaves its grief
Along a broken shore,
And unfolds
Its old-new blue
Under a timeless
Awestruck day,
Far beyond its roar.

AFTERNOON IN MAY

A whale? Basking shark?
Something like a supple log,
The colour of rock,
Brownish, greyish, trawls its way
Through the Big Sur waves.
Seen, unseen, then seen, unseen.

NIGHT DREAM

Unfolding, unfolding
Night dream;
Its slow-rushing, slow-rushing
Moments
Fondle
Black rock and earth,
Tongue the pockets
Of caves.
Its coming, coming
Movements
Hold sky and land
In a spell,
Torment a hard stirring
Of stars,
Lick the moon with its breath,
As it spills
The love semen of aeons.

The View from the Main Window in the Cabin

CABIN VIEW

In the window
Waves foam
To their end;
In my mind
Words form
Their beginning.

SEER

(for Carolyn)

Your home
Nestles
On a cliff-edge
Hill
That rests
Its rocky feet
In a turquoise sea.

Poet, artist,
Ancient
Spirit
As young as Eve,
Star-stirred
Seer;
Blessed woman
Whose kindness
Like the day
Has somewhere
To go,
Your words ride
The burning waves
And your colours
Flame
The broken story.

A DAY OUT
(for Carolyn and John)

We drive
The fast
Road
Along
Big Sur,
The frayed
Coast
Scolded
By the shock
Of the sea;
Armies
Of waves
Bringing
Their weapon
Of blue.
Islands
Of rock
Tower
In swirling
Water,
Like
Ancient
Pillars
Built up
To the gods,
Under
A sky
That's wrecked
By some clouds.
We drive
As if
There is no
Tomorrow;
The sleek jeep
Swallowing
The laid-back
Miles.

DEAR ARTIST
(for Carolyn)

You bring me flowers;
Irises as fragile
As the heart
Of Van Gogh,
And roses
As white as a canvas
Untouched.

MIDNIGHT WALK

Our finger-size torches
Search the dusty path,
As we talk our way
Towards the sea
Panting heavily
Inside the darkness.

Above, the sky is opened
Out, black with eternity,
Boasting a white rash
Of fugitive stars.

THE FAMILY
(for Scott and Linda)

The gorgeous waves break
On the beautiful shore,
Perfectly timed,
Lovely and rhythmic;

Yet it's the smiles
From the family
I meet down the path
That shine like a heaven

And reach to my soul.

MORNING MIST

Big Sur smokes in a mist,
The ocean has gone
For a few strange hours,
Until the ancient shroud
Drifts, magically lifts,
And the bay glistens
And boils in the sun.

Inside the Cabin

LUNCH BREAK IN THE CABIN
(for John Dotson)

Bob Dylan blares
In the cabin,
Pledging his time;
And the ocean's
Regular rhyme
Disappears;
But its movement,
A hypnotic
Stirring slumber,
In the window,
Still holds my gaze.

A View of Big Sur

SONG FROM BIG SUR

Will I ever
Enter
My lover again,
Feel the ocean
Go in
And the ocean
Go out,
And the storm-stunned
Islands
Ride the night?

Will I ever
Feel
The rise
And the fall,
The gasps
And last waves
Of a biblical
Love?

Will I ever
Collapse
On the mountains
Of dawn,
Thirsty
And worn
By the blood
Of her sun?

Will I ever
Lie
On the fire
Of her sand,
Broken
And whole
In the skies
Of her eyes,
Humbled and small
In her castaway hands?

READING D. H. LAWRENCE

You tell me
You're reading
D. H. Lawrence,

Until the early
Hours of the morning.
And I imagine

You in your bed
In the mansion
Perched on a hill

Above this cabin,
Where I write
Into the morning;

Your tiring eyes
Following
The film of his language,

As he draws
You nearer
To the fire

Of emotions,
The pagan flames
Of passion,

The mine-deep drama
Of men
And women.

I imagine
You reading
Until sleep

Darkly aches
In your body,
Puts its dream dust

In your eyes,
As dawn
Unbolts the day,

And Eden's light probes
With fresh fingers
The cave of your room.

WHILST READING DE CASSERES'
The Superman in America
Spinoza, Liberator of God and Man

In the cabin:
No radio,
No T.V.,
Only a player
For CDs;
My usual world
Is somewhere else;

Still selling the dream,
The sale of the soul,
The YOU in the crowd
Still herded by the few,
The fit-in-with-fashion,
Money-gaoled,
Media-fearing,
Emotions on ration,
Flag-confirmed,
Mind-controlled,
Satisfied,
Dissatisfied,
Mechanical
Self.

BIRTHDAY POEM: THE BOY AND THE MAN

'We go toward ourselves' — Benjamin De Casseres
in *Chameleon, Being a Book of My Selves*

The boy on Kilvey
Is the man on Big Sur;
Both humbled by the land
And the sea's vast engine;
Both letting the clouds
Start thoughts in their mind;
Both feeling the trees
Root into their tongue;
Both caged by the birds
That grieve in a trance;
Both walking the tracks
Of the living, the dead;
Both blown by a wind
Like the breath of a god;
Both feeling the sun
Burn all that is born;
Both dressing their ghosts
With the songs from their heart.

One of the Walks Near the Cabin

BIRTHDAY WALK

Walking the dazzling rim
Of the Pacific,
The Grecian-blue sea
And mythological rocks,
I feel the mortal
And sense the eternal.

I am a child
At the window of wonder,
A man spellbound
By a living prayer.

To begin
To imagine
Just one breath of God
Is to attempt
To place a tiger
On the back of an ant.

I stand and I watch
The ocean
Making love
To the humbled bay.

BIRTHDAY AND ALDOUS HUXLEY

On my fifty-ninth birthday
With you in Big Sur,
We watch a film
In a cave of a room
In your mansion of wood,
On a screen the size
Of a cabin wall.

It's Aldous Huxley
(You knew his wife, Laura)
In an interview
From some archive,
A film as old
As the first moon-landing.

He takes us on
A journey
Of marvellous thoughts;
Dignified, profound,
Intelligent, and wise;

And behind us
You lie on your bed,
Unwell,
Frail and as sad
As Elizabeth Browning.

THE BIRD OF GRIEF
a painting by Carolyn Mary Kleefeld

This is the bird of grief
Attended by her ghosts;
Her long black wing outstretched
Like a psalm of sorrow.

All the hurt of man
Is weeping from her eye,
All the war of loving
Is breaking in her night.

This is the room's last shadow,
The mother-feathered pain;
This is the touch of nursing souls
Before the flight of change.

This is the bird of grief
That shrieks inside the blood,
Whose silence is the sound of death,
Whose talons are for love.

The Wood Stove in the Cabin

STORM

(for Stanley H. Barkan)

This cabin
Is at sea;
A small wooden boat
Riding the whips
Of the bullying wind,
Washed by the waves
Of the nailing rain.

The torn coast submits
To the trawling mist,
The window is blistered
With round wounds of water.

I stare
As the new fire
Flares,
Its magic
Shredding the logs
With fondling fingers
Of yellow and red;

Till I sit by a legend
Of ancient
Comfort.

LATER

Later, at the table,
From a stockpile of old thoughts,
A bundle of dry words
And yesterday's dark news,
A poem catches fire.

BIRDMAN

I meet this man
Who paints birds,
Beautifully,
Tenderly;
They could fly
From the flat cage
Of each frame.

"Send them out,"
I suggest,
"A display–
Like a poet
Sends out his singing words."

He raises
His shoulders,
Like a hawk
Disturbed
By a movement
In the mind,

Turns away,
And nests
Inside
His silence.

YOUR BLUE EYES CALL ME
(for Patricia)

Your blue eyes
Call me
Back to Atlantis;

Where seahorses
Rode
An ecstatic dream;

Where the corals
Were treasures
Too rich for a queen;

Where our thoughts
Were like rainbows
That necklace the sun;

Where the golden days
Danced with the souls
Of our world;

Where the nights
Were lit up
Like Aladdin's cave.

Your blue eyes
Call me
To a world

We have lost;
A peace in our minds,
In our bodies

And our hearts.
Your blue eyes
Call me

To a place
We have lost,
Except

For the feelings
In memory's
Dust.

Big Sur Sculptor Edmund Kara's Derelict Cabin

BIG SUR SCULPTOR EDMUND KARA'S
DERELICT CABIN

Time and again,
On my daily walks,
I'm drawn to your home,
Your workshop lodged
Just above the Pacific.

It's as if I'm called,
Pulled by the bare soul
Of your broken place,
A shrine of dark wood,
Quickly eroding
On the nerves of the weather,
In the slow mouth
Of time as it gnaws.

I walk down the path
Once worn by your shadow.
Today, as I approach
It looks even sadder;
As I enter one door
Another one whines
Through its old wound
To the heart-aching sea,
Which is crashing
Relentlessly
At this world where you worked.

Fragments of the windows
Litter the deck floor.
They're as sharp as the tools
You once used to shape
Truths into wood:
And wood into truths.

The fireplace, it seems,
Is waiting for the flames
To warm a dead room
With a sudden hearth's blaze.

You became a recluse,
Shunning art's game
And the ego's long thirst,
Like a castaway
On an island
Alone with his dream.

Outside, I pass
The stark KEEP OUT,
Which the dangerous
And determined
Elements ignore.

Note: Emund Kara, sculptor, is particularly famous for his nude sculpture of Elizabeth Taylor, which is featured in the film *The Sandpiper*, starring her and Richard Burton.

AN INSOMNIAC'S MORNING

The sea grinds its oaths
On the body of the day;
The sun is hiding
Beyond a bruise of cold clouds.

Some words start to shine
In a junkyard of feelings.

The Dusty Road to the Cabin

CONVOY OF TRUCKS, BIG SUR

They spray a beige dust
As they trundle toward me
On the dirt-rough road.

Each driver waves as his truck
Ploughs clouds into the morning.

MID-DAY WAVES

The snowy-tipped force
Of each wave swimming across,
Sperming the whole bay.

THE WIND

I heard the wind
Before I woke;
I heard the wind
As I woke;
It warned
The world of its wound,
It seemed
Bothered by a day
It was blowing
Away.

Elephant Seals, Big Sur

ELEPHANT SEALS
(for Carolyn and John)

They loll just like an unruly army,
Tired and stressed by their sea-playing day.

A colony of overweight, naked
Colonels; *Mirounga angustirostris*;

Living logs, oiled-up and stone-rock coloured
Blubber, they huddle like a dying herd

Of couch-size maggots. They burp and shriek:
A strange pantomime at the ocean's edge.

Gregarious sunbathers now wind-blown;
One flicks up sand, as two others stretch high

And aggressively fawn, a ritual,
As they bite and show their salmon-pink throats.

Some check our presence with doleful eyes,
Others grossly crawl-flap to the water;

One elegantly moves through satin waves;
Several, farther out, head-bob around

Like bald men basking in holiday sun.
A weird sculpture sprawled out on the shore,

Performance art by drunken aliens,
They move and moan, an abandoned lament;

A shipwreck of creatures overlapping
Their woes, they litter the place like loafers.

Part-comic, part-tragic, they lie behind
Big Sur's fast road and the thrill-seeking cars.

The Front View of the Cabin

THE CABIN
(for Vince Clemente)

A monk's cell, wooden,
Squatting above the ocean,
Big Sur's shattered coast.
Like an Egyptian god's eye,
The main window holds, each day,
The stained-glass blue sea,
Jigsaw-piece cliffs, proud mountains
Touching gathered clouds
That are white as cotton-wool;
And, always, the waves coming
To gasp on the shore.

Each night the window's picture
Is shadowed; the sea,
The cliffs, the mountains, charcoaled
By the cloud of night;
And, always, the waves coming
To gasp on the shore.

LEAVING

Did I sleep
Into a dream,
Or step on to a set
Of a film being made?

As I pack to leave
It all seems so unreal;
A Spinoza illusion,
A De Casseres mist,
In this cabin
On Big Sur,
On the shelf
Of an ocean,

Endlessly weaving
Its haunting rhythms,
Endlessly making
Its mind-moving myth.

CODA

1. The Sea of Big Sur

The sea insists
On an old rag of a song,
As a lone boat
Is bashed by a bay of a wind.

The sea persists with its
Kettledrum throng, a waterfall
Gong calling a storm.

Bones, bedded
In the cellar of time,
Moan and groan;
Their surfaced cries
Thrash the walls of the world.

The sighs of fathers
And sons rise
From below
To bellow and blow
In the loveless night.

Waves argue over rocks
And knock on the doors
Of the clouds.

Each breath of the sea
Is heavier
Than a whale;
Each movement of its force
Is sleeker than a shark.

Water praising the boom of its phrases;
Water banging
El Sur grande;
Haranguing time
With its life and its death.

A commotion
Of emotion; a rhythm
Unfolding;
Battle chants battering
The Earth's sleeping face.

It is the sea of Big Sur,
Stirred in a thought
More vast than the sky.

It is the sea of Big Sur,
Shadowed by the soul
Of the moon,
Erasing the flesh
Of the land.

It is not even a moment
In the mood
Of the mind of creation,
This ocean washing
The bowl of a dream.

2. Thoughts on the Way to San Francisco Airport

All thoughts brush away
The old cobwebs of a faith.
The mind is a sky
At night, teeming with stars.
Creation's abandoned dream?
Or cells replicating hope?

No stone-built place can
Bring you to your knees.
Time is a shadow of you;
Aeons are moments,
A mere one pulse
To the slow mathematics
Of your each movement;
And being is believing.

Peter Viewing Big Sur

ABOUT THE AUTHOR

Peter Thabit Jones was born in Swansea, Wales, and raised by his grandparents. His first American book of poems, *The Lizard Catchers*, published by New York publisher Cross-Cultural Communications in 2006, is now in its third edition. His poem "Kilvey Hill" has been incorporated into a permanent stained-glass window in the new Saint Thomas Community School in Swansea, Wales. The window is the work of leading stained-glass artist Catrin Jones of Wales. Peter toured America, with Aeronwy Thomas, daughter of Dylan Thomas, for six weeks in March 2008, giving readings and workshops from New York to California. The tour was organized by Stanley H. Barkan of Cross-Cultural Communications. He has tutored Children's Literature, Adult Literature, and Creative Writing for the Adult Education Department at Swansea University, Wales, for seventeen years.

Peter is the founder and editor of *The Seventh Quarry/Swansea Poetry Magazine*, which is published in Swansea, Wales, with an international perspective. It was awarded Second Best Small Press Magazine Award 2006 by the Annual Purple Patch UK Awards.

His poem "Bereavement," from his American book *The Lizard Catchers*, was one of the poems broadcast on September 11, 2007, on The North Sea Poetry Scene's *Art Forum* television program on Cablevision Public Access Channel 20, Long Island, New York.

Peter was invited to Serbia, in September 2006, by the Serbian Writers' Association, to participate in the XLIIIrd International Meeting of Writers in Belgrade. He was visiting poet in Romania in 2008 and 2009. His poems have been translated into over twenty languages, including Arabic, Bengali, Catalan, Chinese, Dutch, French, German, Hebrew, Italian, Japanese, Korean, Persian, Portuguese, Romanian, Russian, Serbian, Tagalog, and Turkish.

A bilingual English-Romanian collection of poems, *A Bucket of Sky,* translated by Dr. Olimpia Iacob, is forthcoming in Romania. A 200-page bilingual collection (English-Romanian), *Whispers of the Soul*, featuring poems by Peter and America's Vince Clemente, also translated by Dr. Olimpia Iacob, was published in Romania in 2008.

Peter is the recipient of several awards for his work, including the Eric Gregory Award for Poetry (The Society of Authors, London), The Society of Authors Award (London), The Royal Literary Fund Award (London), and an Arts Council of Wales Award (Wales). He has been a prize-winner in several UK and international poetry competitions.

His poem "I Want to Be an Astronaut" was used in the U.K. Government's English Curriculum for all SECONDARY SCHOOL ANNUAL EXAMINATIONS 2006.

Peter has written, with Aeronwy Thomas, the daughter of Dylan Thomas, the first-ever *Dylan Thomas Walking Tour of Greenwich Village, New York* (2008) for the Wales International Centre, New York/Welsh Assembly Government.

He was appointed the organizer in Wales for a new Creative Writing/Cultural project with Knox College, America, the Carl Sandburg Birthplace, America, Cross-Cultural Communications, America, the Wales International Center, America, and his magazine *The Seventh Quarry/Swansea Poetry Magazine*. The project, Dylan Thomas in Wales/American Students Visiting Project, was launched in March 2010.

Peter returned to America twice in 2009, to attend the World Affairs Conference in Boulder, Colorado, and to film a DVD version of the *Dylan Thomas Walking Tour of Greenwich Village in New York*, with him as narrator. He visited America for six weeks in April and May 2010 for a third tour organized by Stanley H. Barkan. He gave readings in New York and then traveled to Carmel and Monterey, California, for several poetry readings with Stanley, Carolyn Mary Kleefeld, and John Dotson, who organised the events with Patricia Holt. The world-premiere performance of his verse drama, *The Boy and the Lion's Head*, directed by John Dotson, with music by Martin Shears, took place in Monterey. He resided at Big Sur for the whole month of May as a writer-in-residence.

Further information: www.peterthabitjones.com

Peter's Desk in the Cabin on Big Sur